EVERYDAY SCIENCE

about

your toys

Barbara Taylor

photography by
Peter Millard

MACDONALD YOUNG BOOKS

First published in 1996
by Macdonald Young Books
61 Western Road
Hove
East Sussex
BN3 1JD

Text © Barbara Taylor 1996
Illustration © Macdonald Young Books 1996

Commissioning editor: Debbie Fox

Project editor: Caroline Wilson

Design: The Design Works, Reading

Illustrators: David Pattison, Martin Woodward

The publisher and author would like to thank Carol
Olivier of Kenmont Primary School, and the
following children for taking part in the
photography: Charlene Airey, Scott
Archer-Nicholls, Michael
Augustine, Danny
Botross, Daniel Furby,
Natalie Gashi, Jake
Hinckson, Mikey
Martinez, Tanika Swaby,
Leanne Thomas, Christina
Toboas and Samantha Wallace.

Thanks also to Beatty Hallas, BRIO Ltd,
Fisher-Price Toys UK Ltd, Halfords,
LEGO UK Ltd, Early Learning Centre.
Barbie is a registered trademark
of Mattel Toys.
Meccano is a registered trademark.

Printed and Bound in Portugal by:
Edições ASA

A CIP catalogue record for this
book is available from the British
Library.

ISBN 0 7500 1988 3

Contents

What makes my car go? 4
Why do I have to wind up my toy frog?

**Why is my pogo
stick springy?** 5
Why can I bounce high
on my hopper?

**Why does my
electronic game light up?** 6
Why don't the pieces fall off my travel game?

How can I make my train go faster? 7
Which ends of my trains stick together?

**How does my computer
know where to move?** 8
What's inside my computer?

**How does the mouse move
things on my screen?** 9

How far can I hit my baseball? 10
Why is the slide so slippery?

**How can I stop
on my rollerblades?** 11
How can I score a goal in table soccer?

**Why do my marbles zoom fast down
my marble run?** 12
Why is my car heavier than my truck?

**How high will my ball
bounce?** 13

**How does my toy
crane lift things?** 14
Why does my bulldozer have caterpillar tracks?

Why does my spade make
it easier to dig? 15
How can I make a see-saw balance?

Why does my bike have
rough tyres? 16
Why do gears make it
easier to go uphill?

How does my
cycle helmet
protect my head? 17

Why does my tent
have a curved shape? 18
Why is the climbing frame so strong?

How high can I build
my space shuttle tower? 19
Why do Meccano pieces have holes in them?

Why does a frisbee
fly through the air? 20
Why does my model plane glide a long way?

Why does my dinghy float? 21
How can I steer my speedboat?

Why do the patterns change as I turn
my kaleidoscope? 22
Why are my marbles see-through?

How do the pictures
get on to the film in my camera? 23
Why do my stars glow in the dark?

How can my friend hear me on his
walkie-talkie? 24
How does the music get on to my party tape?

How does my keyboard
make different notes? 25
Why do I need to cover the holes on my recorder?

Why are all the bits for my model
car kit joined together? 26
Why does my action doll's head twist around?

Why does my teddy growl? 27
How does the stuffing get inside my teddy?

Why do I need to mix my face
paints with water? 28
Why do my felt pens dry
out when I leave the lids off?

Why does my
modelling clay go
hard? 29
Why is glue sticky?

More about the science of toys 30

Index and quiz answers 32

Toy safety

- Switch off your computer when you are not using it. This saves energy and stops the computer getting too hot.
- Take the batteries out of your toys if you are not using them for a while. Poisonous chemicals may leak out of old batteries.
- You should wear a helmet plus knee and elbow pads when you ride your bike or skate on your rollerblades. They will protect you from knocks and grazes.
- If you play with an inflatable boat at the seaside, make sure an adult is holding it firmly. You could quickly be swept out to sea.

What makes my car go?

When you move the controls on the hand-set of your remote-control car, it sends radio signals to the car. The aerial on the car picks up the signals and they make tiny electric motors work inside the car. These motors make the car move. The motors are driven by the electricity made by the batteries. Electricity is a kind of energy, which makes things happen.

Why do I have to wind up my toy frog?

When you turn the key of a wind-up toy, you tighten a spring inside it. This stores energy in the spring. When you take the key out, or let go of it, the spring unwinds, giving the toy the energy to move.

Did you know that millions of the world's smallest batteries would fit on the tip of your finger?

Why is my pogo stick springy?

When you push down on the foot-bar of a pogo stick, you squash the spring. As you jump up, the spring stretches out again very quickly, helping you to bounce up into the air. When a material goes back into shape after being squashed or stretched, it is called an elastic material. The particles that make up an elastic material can be pushed together or pulled apart, but they always go back to where they started.

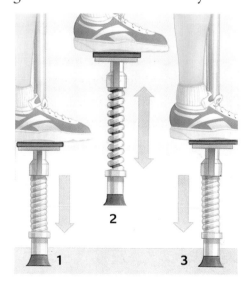

1 and **3** Pushing down with your feet forces the coils in the spring closer together and stores energy in the spring. **2** Jumping up lets the coils spring apart again, releasing the energy that pushes you up into the air.

Why can I bounce high on my hopper?

Hoppers are full of air, which keeps squashing together and stretching out again as you bounce up and down. The rubber 'skin' of the hopper is elastic too.

Did you know that King Tutankhamun played with toys nearly 4,000 years ago in Ancient Egypt?

Why don't the pieces fall off my travel game?

The pieces stick to the board because they are magnetic. Even if you turn the board upside down, the pieces will not fall off. This is because the pieces give off an invisible force which pulls some materials towards them.

Why does my electronic game light up?

The batteries inside the game make electricity, or electrical energy, by mixing chemicals together. The electrical energy from the batteries is turned into light energy to make the circles light up. Electricity has to move along wires inside the game to make it work. The batteries push the electricity along the wires.

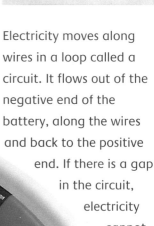

battery

electricity makes bulb glow

paper clip touches drawing pin to close gap in circuit

Electricity moves along wires in a loop called a circuit. It flows out of the negative end of the battery, along the wires and back to the positive end. If there is a gap in the circuit, electricity cannot flow.

Which ends of my trains stick together?

The silver magnets on the train and its carriages are not all the same. There are two different kinds. If two magnets that are different are held together, they will stick to each other. If the two magnets are the same, they will push each other away.

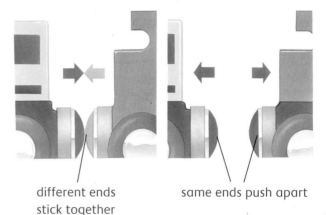

different ends stick together

same ends push apart

How can I make my train go faster?

An electric train like this one is pushed along by the energy from an electric motor inside the engine. The motor picks up electricity from wires in the track and changes the electricity into movement. Turning the yellow dial on the transformer unit changes the amount of electricity in the track. With more electricity, the train goes faster. With less electricity, it goes more slowly.

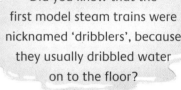

Did you know that the first model steam trains were nicknamed 'dribblers', because they usually dribbled water on to the floor?

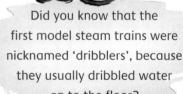

How does my computer know where to move?

A computer contains sets of instructions called programs, which tell it how to carry out particular tasks. People have to feed these programs into the computer, because it cannot work things out for itself like you can. In a computer game like this one, the program contains examples of lots of possible moves. The computer chooses the one that best follows your move.

What's inside my computer?

There are three main parts: a chip called a central processing unit, or CPU for short, which is the control centre of the computer; the memory chips; and hard magnetic disks or floppy disks which store programs and data. Computer chips store programs and information as electronic signals.

Did you know that a virtual reality game makes you feel as if you really are in another 3D world, perhaps out in space?

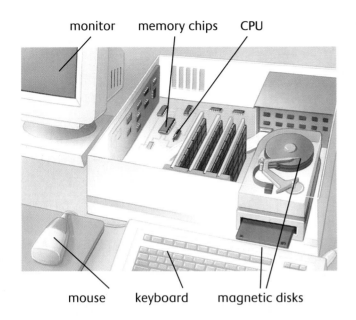

monitor   memory chips   CPU

mouse   keyboard   magnetic disks

How does the mouse move things on my screen?

As you move the mouse over a mat or desk-top, electric signals from the mouse tell the computer how far the mouse has moved and in which direction it has moved. The computer then moves the cursor on the screen in the same direction as the mouse. By 'marking' pictures and words with the cursor, you can move them around on the screen. When you stop the cursor on an icon and click the mouse switch, the computer will carry out the task the icon stands for.

True or false?

1 Computers that play chess can 'think' about 700,000 positions per second.

2 The first computer mice used to squeak instead of click when you pressed them.

3 A memory chip is as thin as a hair and no bigger than a shirt button.

4 One CD ROM disk can store as many words as there are in 1,000 paperback books.

The answers are on page 32.

The answers are on page 32.

Did you know that some baseball players can throw the ball as fast as 145 kph? The ball goes from the pitcher to the batter in less than half a second!

Why is the slide so slippery?

The slide is very smooth and shiny so there is not much to catch against your clothes and hold you back. When one thing slides over another, the force that tries to slow down or stop the movement is called friction.

How far can I hit my baseball?

The harder you hit the baseball, the further it will go. The push that you use to hit the ball when you swing the bat is a kind of force. The bat makes the force much bigger. Forces are invisible, like energy. You can only see what they do to things. The baseball will keep moving fast in a straight line, and will not stop until someone catches it or it hits the ground.

How can I stop on my rollerblades?

You need to use a pushing force to stop the wheels from rolling along. The brake on the back of some rollerblades makes this easier, especially if you lift the wheels off the ground. Friction helps to slow you down and it gets stronger as the pressure between two surfaces increases. The harder you press on the brake, the faster you stop. The energy you use to brake comes from the chemical energy stored in your muscles.

Did you know that the first roller skates had no brakes? In 1760, the inventor skated into a ballroom playing the violin, and crashed into a huge mirror!

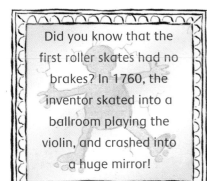

How can I score a goal in table soccer?

In table soccer, you need to push or pull the players into different positions to make the ball move or stop, go faster or slower or change direction – and score a goal! Pushes and pulls like these are called forces.

Why is my car heavier than my truck?

Your toys have weight because of gravity pulling them down. Their exact weight depends on their size and the materials they are made of. A small metal car may be heavier than a large plastic truck, because it is made of a heavier material.

Why do my marbles zoom fast down my marble run?

The marbles roll downwards because a force called gravity pulls everything on Earth down to the ground. The channels are smooth and shiny to cut down any friction holding back the marbles. This makes them zoom down really fast, especially where the channels lead downwards at a steep angle. When you lift the marbles up to the top of the run again, you have to overcome the downward force of gravity.

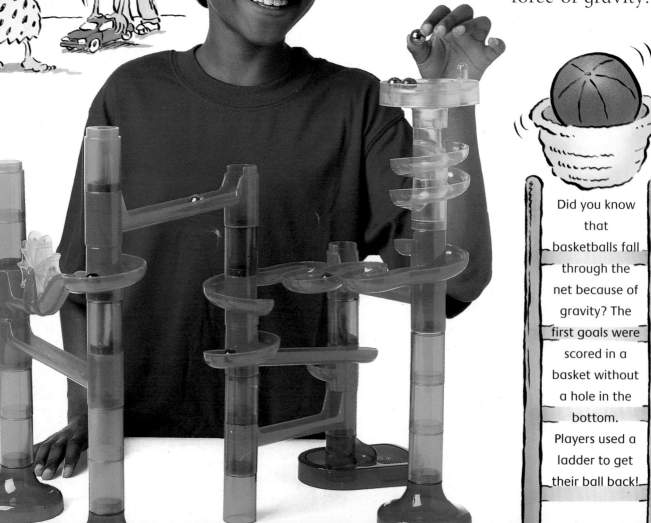

Did you know that basketballs fall through the net because of gravity? The first goals were scored in a basket without a hole in the bottom. Players used a ladder to get their ball back!

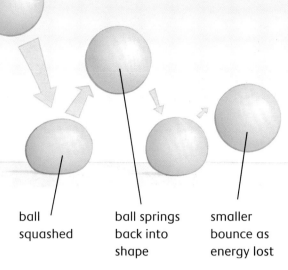

ball
squashed

ball springs
back into
shape

smaller
bounce as
energy lost

A ball bounces a little bit lower each time.
No ball ever bounces all the way back. If it did,
it would go on bouncing for ever. On each
bounce, some energy is lost as sound and
heat, leaving less energy for the next bounce.

How high will my ball bounce?

The harder you throw a ball to the ground, the higher it bounces. Balls bounce because of the springiness or elasticity of the material they are made of, as well as the springy air trapped inside. If a ball loses some air, it won't bounce as high. When a ball hits the ground, the bottom part is squashed and stores energy. As the ball springs back into shape, it pushes itself off the ground.

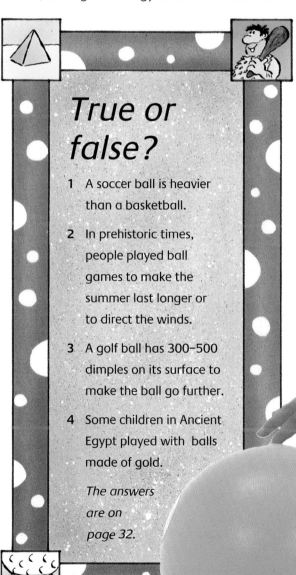

True or false?

1   A soccer ball is heavier than a basketball.

2   In prehistoric times, people played ball games to make the summer last longer or to direct the winds.

3   A golf ball has 300–500 dimples on its surface to make the ball go further.

4   Some children in Ancient Egypt played with balls made of gold.

The answers are on page 32.

Did you know that a leather soccer ball is made of 32 panels stitched together?

Why does my bulldozer have caterpillar tracks?

Caterpillar tracks help a real bulldozer to climb up steep banks and move smoothly over bumps. They also stop bulldozers sinking into soft, muddy ground because they spread out the weight of the bulldozer over a bigger area than wheels would do.

How does my toy crane lift things?

The toy crane has a pulley wheel, which is a wheel with a groove for the thread to fit into. In real life, a rope or a metal cable runs through a pulley wheel. To lift the toy car *up*, you have to pull the thread around the pulley wheel *down*. So a pulley with one wheel changes the direction of the pulling force. Pulleys make it easier to lift things straight up because it is easier to pull a rope down than to lift a weight up.

Did you know that the name LEGO comes from the Danish words, 'leg godt', which mean 'play well'?

How can I make a see-saw balance?

If there are two children who weigh roughly the same sitting on either end of a see-saw, it will balance. The same amount of force will be pressing down on the see-saw at each end.

Two children have to sit about halfway between the end of the see-saw and the middle to balance one child sitting on the other end.

Did you know that lots of your toys are levers or have levers inside them? These include puppets, bikes, bats, diggers and see-saws.

Why does my spade make it easier to dig?

A spade is a sort of lever, which is a simple machine that allows a small force – the effort – to overcome a larger force – the load. A lever is a stiff rod or bar that turns about a fixed point, called a pivot or fulcrum, in order to move a load. When you push down on the handle of the spade (the effort) the blade moves up and lifts the soil (the load). When the blade is in the soil, the pivot is where the blade joins the handle. The higher your hands are up the handle, the easier it is to lift the soil.

Why does my bike have rough tyres?

Mountain bike tyres have a rough pattern on them called the tread. This increases the friction between the tyres and the ground and makes the tyres grip instead of sliding about. In wet weather, water slides into the grooves in the tread and sprays out from under the wheels. This helps to stop the bike from skidding. Racing bike tyres have smooth wheels that roll around very fast, but do not grip well, especially if the roads are wet or icy.

Why do gears make it easier to go uphill?

To cycle uphill, you use a big gear wheel. This turns the back wheel slowly, but with more pushing force. To go downhill, you use a small gear wheel, which turns the wheel quickly, but with less force. This lets the bike travel fast downhill or along the flat.

The longest bike ever built had seats for 35 people and was over 20 metres long!

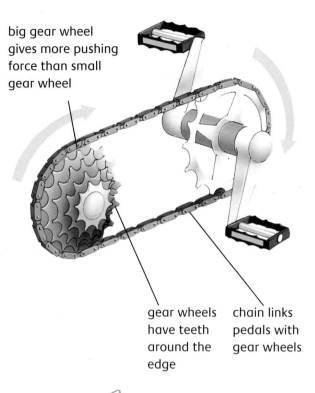

big gear wheel gives more pushing force than small gear wheel

gear wheels have teeth around the edge

chain links pedals with gear wheels

True or false?

1 The first bikes did not have pedals.

2 Penny farthing bicycles were named after two British coins.

3 There are ten times as many bikes as cars in the world.

The answers are on page 32.

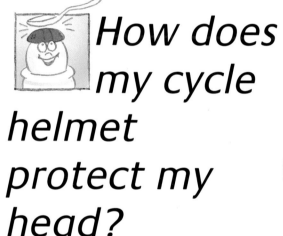 *How does my cycle helmet protect my head?*

The hard surface on the outside of the helmet spreads out the impact of any bumps or knocks. This reduces the pressure on your head. The padding inside stops the helmet from slipping. It also helps to absorb any knocks before they reach your head. Air-vents in the top of the helmet keep your head cool.

Why does my tent have a curved shape?

A curved shape spreads out the force of the tightly stretched material pushing downwards and inwards. This means there is not a lot of pressure on one point. A curved shape is also good at supporting its own weight. It can reach across a large space, leaving you lots of room to play.

pushing force goes down poles into the ground

This tent stands up on its own without any ropes or pegs to stretch it into shape and hold it still. The flexible poles will bend a lot without breaking.

Why is the climbing frame so strong?

The tubes that make up a climbing frame are strong, but light. They can stand up to a lot of force pressing down on them from above. The shape of a climbing frame is also important. Triangular shapes inside the frame are strong because they keep their shape well and do not twist and collapse under pressure.

How high can I build my space shuttle tower?

Piles of smooth toy bricks easily fall over. But the studs on LEGO bricks cleverly fit into tubes on other pieces, making it easier to build the bricks into tall, rigid structures.

To make a tall tower, the bricks have to be snapped together one on top of the other, so the weight pushes straight down through all the bricks. If the bottom of the tower is wider than the top, it helps to spread out the pressure above and make a firmer structure. LEGO towers 20 metres high have been built with about 300,000 bricks!

Why do Meccano pieces have holes in them?

The holes in pieces of Meccano let you join the pieces together with nuts and bolts in many different ways. So one set of Meccano can make lots of different toys, from cars and cranes to towers and aeroplanes.

Why does my model plane glide a long way?

The wings of your model plane are an aerofoil shape – curved on top and almost flat underneath. This makes a difference in air pressure above and below the wing – low pressure above and high pressure below. Like a frisbee, the plane is pushed up into the air and glides a long way before landing.

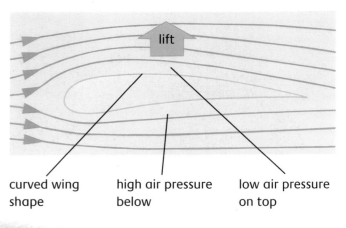

lift

curved wing shape

high air pressure below

low air pressure on top

The first frisbees were empty pie tins from the Frisbie bakery in North America. They were called 'Morrison's flyin' saucers', but the name didn't catch on!

Why does a frisbee fly through the air?

A frisbee cannot fly on its own. When you throw the frisbee, the pushing force from your muscles launches it into the air. Once it is in the air, the special curved top of the frisbee makes the air flow faster over the top than underneath. Air above the frisbee presses on it less than the air below. The frisbee is lifted up towards the low air pressure. The smooth shape of the frisbee does not catch against the air, and this helps it to glide along fast.

Why does my dinghy float?

You have to pump a lot of air into the sides of a dinghy before you can sit in it and row along. The air makes the dinghy light, even though it is quite big. As it floats, the dinghy pushes some water out of the way. This water pushes back against the bottom of the boat, holding it up on the surface. The weight of the dinghy pushing down is the same as the force of the water pushing up.

How can I steer my speedboat?

A toy speedboat may have a rudder at the back of the boat. This sticks down into the water and has a handle so you can turn it from side to side. When you push the rudder one way, the water pushes the boat in the other direction.

Why do the patterns change as I turn my kaleidoscope?

When you look into a kaleidoscope, you see lots of little coloured shapes. Inside the kaleidoscope, light bounces to and fro between the smooth, shiny surfaces. This is called reflection. You see lots of reflections of one set of shapes, so the same pattern is repeated many times. As you turn the ring, the shapes move and the pattern changes.

Why are my marbles see-through?

Some marbles are made from clear glass, which lets light pass through so you can see through them. They are called transparent. Other marbles are made of glass that you cannot see through, and are called opaque. Shadows form behind opaque materials because the light cannot go through them. Light always travels in straight lines so it cannot bend around the marbles to light up the dark shadow area.

How do the pictures get on to the film in my camera?

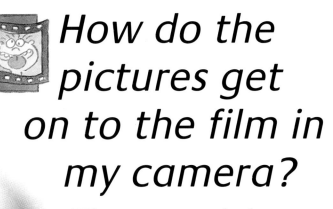

button to open shutter

shutter

viewfinder to see photo you are taking

lens to direct light on to film

aperture

film

When you press the button to take a photo, a door called a shutter opens for a split second. This lets light coming from the person or scene you are looking at through to the film inside the camera When this light hits the film, it makes a picture of the person or scene on the film.

When you are not using your camera, the shutter is closed and stops light getting on to the film. When you take a photo, the shutter opens, and light comes through a hole called the aperture on to the film.

Why do my stars glow in the dark?

Stick-on stars glow in the dark because they take in an invisible kind of light, called ultraviolet light, and give out a kind of light that we can see. When one kind of light is changed into another kind of light, this is called fluorescence.

How can my friend hear me on his walkie-talkie?

The sound of your voice is changed into electrical signals inside your walkie-talkie. These electrical signals make your aerial give off radio signals in all directions. The aerial on your friend's walkie-talkie picks up the radio signals, which are changed back into electrical signals inside his walkie-talkie. The electrical signals cause movement in the walkie-talkie's speaker. This makes the air shake to produce an exact copy of the sound of your voice.

How does the music get on to my party tape?

In a recording studio, the sounds of the music make tiny metal particles on the tape move into a particular pattern. The pattern is different for each piece of music. When you play the tape, the pattern makes electrical signals which are changed into sound by a loudspeaker.

stereo tapes have two tracks recorded on the same tape

each piece of music has its own pattern

How does my keyboard make different notes?

Your keyboard produces music from electric signals. When you press the different keys, you change the voltage, which is the force that pushes electricity through wires inside the keyboard. This changes the pitch of the sound, making high or low notes. Other knobs, dials or slides switch different electric circuits on or off, making other changes to the music. The sound of the music comes out of a loudspeaker beside the keyboard.

Why do I need to cover the holes on my recorder?

Your recorder is full of air, which shakes or vibrates, as you blow into the recorder. This makes musical notes. With all the holes covered, you make a long column of air and low notes. Taking your fingers off some holes makes a shorter column of air and higher notes.

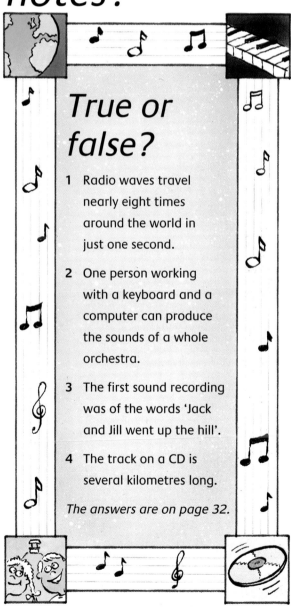

True or false?

1 Radio waves travel nearly eight times around the world in just one second.

2 One person working with a keyboard and a computer can produce the sounds of a whole orchestra.

3 The first sound recording was of the words 'Jack and Jill went up the hill'.

4 The track on a CD is several kilometres long.

The answers are on page 32.

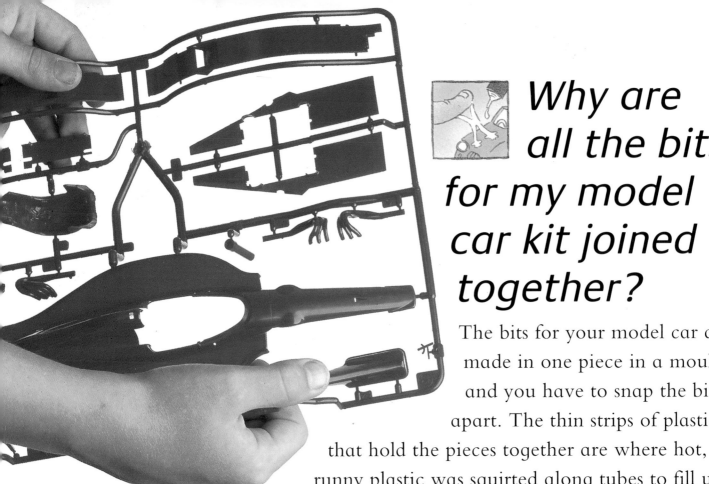

Why are all the bits for my model car kit joined together?

The bits for your model car are made in one piece in a mould and you have to snap the bits apart. The thin strips of plastic that hold the pieces together are where hot, runny plastic was squirted along tubes to fill up the spaces inside the mould. It is cheaper to sell model kits like this because the different parts do not have be broken up, sorted and packed.

Why does my action doll's head twist around ?

The head of an action doll fits on to a plastic ring which sits inside the neck. The ring rolls in all directions, letting your doll twist its head around, as well as tilt it backwards and forwards.

True or false?

1   Teddy bears are named after President Roosevelt of the USA, whose nickname was 'Teddy'.

2   More Barbie dolls and Barbie family members have been made than there are people in the whole world.

3   The amount of fabric used for Barbie's wardrobe would stretch from London to Sydney three times.

4   The first dolls were made of plastic.

The answers are on page 32.

How does the stuffing get inside my teddy?

If a teddy is made by a machine, a nozzle blows the stuffing in through a gap in one of the seams at the back. If the teddy is made by hand, the stuffing has to be pushed in by hand, which takes much longer. Then the seam is sewn up.

Did you know that the first teddy bears were covered in the wool from Angora goats?

Why does my teddy growl?

Your teddy only growls when you turn him upside down or tilt him from side to side. Inside the teddy is a plastic box called a tilt growler. When you move your teddy, a weight in the tilt growler opens or closes some bellows. These push air over strips of metal and plastic called a reed. The reed shakes, making a growling sound.

Why do I need to mix my face paints with water?

Face paints come in hard cakes of pressed powder that will not spread over your skin. When you mix the face paints with water, they flow easily, letting you paint designs such as butterflies, clowns, tigers or even monsters! The paints do not mix with your skin though, they only sit on the surface. As the paints dry, the water disappears into the air, making the paints go hard again. Sometimes, the paints shrink and crack, especially if you put too much on.

Why do my felt pens dry out when I leave the lids off?

The ink used in felt-tip pens contains water. If you leave the lids off your pens, the water disappears into the air, or evaporates, and the pens dry out.

Why is glue sticky?

When you squeeze the glue out of a tube, it meets some moisture in the air and on the surface that it touches. This makes chains of particles in the glue join together to make longer chains. These chains form strong links, like fences, between the surfaces you are sticking together. This holds them firmly together and stops them pulling apart.

Why does my modelling clay go hard?

If you leave your clay models for a while, they dry out, and go quite hard. But some modelling clays can also be cooked or baked in an oven to make them go extra hard. The particles that make up the modelling clay separate and then join together again to form stronger substances. So baked clay is very hard and strong. It doesn't go soft when it gets wet.

More about the science of toys

While you are having fun playing with your toys, you are also finding out about all kinds of science, from forces, flight and floating, to energy, electricity, light and sound. Across these two pages, you can read about some of the most important science ideas in this book.

1 **Energy** makes thing happen. It makes your toys move, make sounds, give out light and get hot.

2 A **force** is usually a push or a pull that makes something start moving, stop moving, change its shape, or change its speed or direction.

3 **Electricity** is a form of energy. An electric current is made up of particles called **electrons**, which move along wires. An unbroken loop along which an electric current flows is called a **circuit**.

4 **Gravity** is an invisible pulling force that pulls things down to the ground and gives them **weight**.

5 A **lever** is made up of a rigid bar and a fixed point, around which it moves, or pivots.

A **pulley wheel** has a groove around the edge to take a cable or rope. As the cable or rope moves, the wheel turns and lifts objects up.

A dinghy **floats** when water pushes up against it with a force called **upthrust**, holding it on the surface.

A wheel with teeth around the edge is called a **gear wheel**. It changes the speed or direction of movement.

6 **Light** is a mixture of electrical and magnetic energy that travels in straight lines. When light bounces off things, this is called **reflection**.

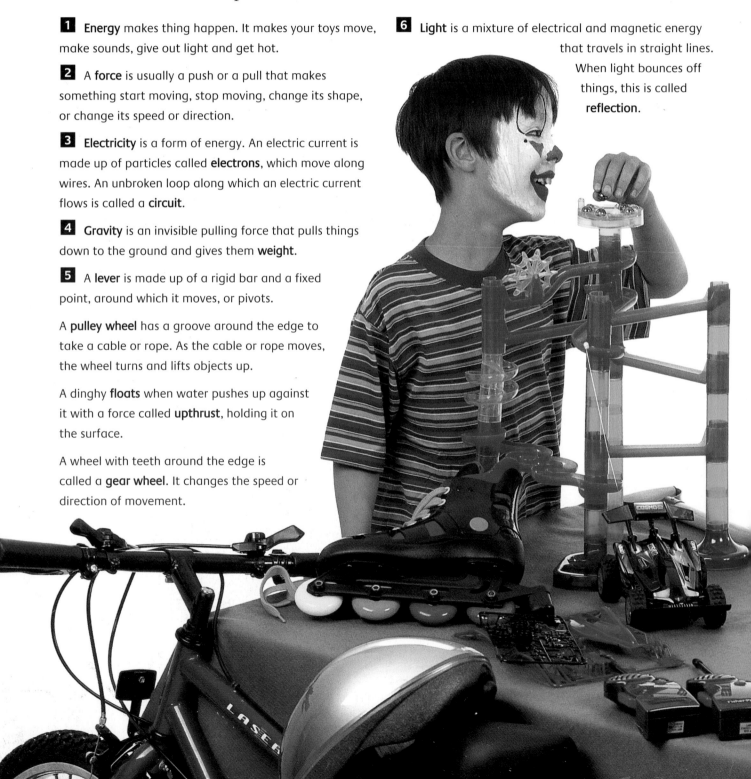

7 Like light, **radio signals** are a mixture of electrical and magnetic energy. They travel at the speed of light, which is 300 million metres per second.

8 A **sound** happens when something shakes or vibrates. Sound travels much more slowly than light or radio signals, at 330 metres per second in air.

The 'highness' or 'lowness' of a sound is called its **pitch**.

Everything is made up of tiny particles called **molecules**.

9 The force of air pressing up against things like toy aeroplanes and keeping them up in the air is called **lift**.

The **chips** which make up a computer consist of very, very tiny electric circuits engraved on tiny chips of silicon.

10 When liquid water **evaporates,** it changes into a gas called water vapour.

11 When two surfaces rub against each other, a force called **friction** slows them down or stops them moving.

12 An **electric motor** is a machine that uses a magnet to change electricity into movement.

Some pieces of metal or stone give off an invisible **magnetic** force that attracts or repels (pushes away) certain materials. The pull of a magnet is stronger at the ends – called the poles.

13 An **elastic** material goes back into shape after being squashed or stretched.

Pressure is the amount of force pressing on a certain area.

14 A **transformer** is used to change the pushing power or **voltage** of an electric current.

15 You can see through **transparent** substances, but you cannot see through **opaque** substances.

Answers to quizzes

Page

9 **1** True. A top player can only think a few moves ahead. Chess computers contain details of hundreds of games played by top chess players; **2** False; **3** True; **4** True.

13 **1** False. A basketball weighs 600 –650g, but a soccer ball weighs only 396–453g; **2** True; **3** True. The dimples make the air flow more smoothly behind the ball, so there is less rough air to catch against the ball and slow it down. They also help to lift the ball and keep it in the air; **4** True.

17 **1** True. Riders pushed them along with their feet. These first bikes were called hobby horses; **2** True. The penny was a big coin and the farthing was a small coin; **3** False. There are only twice as many bikes as cars in the world.

25 **1** True. Radio waves travel at the speed of light, which is faster than anything else in the universe; **2** True; **3** False. It was 'Mary had a little lamb...', spoken by Thomas Edison in 1877; **4** True.

26 **1** True. He once saved a real bear cub on a hunting trip and toy-makers saw their chance to sell cuddly bears and make a lot of money; **2** False. But twice as many Barbies have been made than there are people in the whole USA; **3** True. About 91,000 km of fabric has been used since 1959; **4** False. Plastics have only been around for about 40 years and the first dolls were made thousands of years ago out of clay or wood.

A
Action dolls, 26
Aerofoils, 20

B
Balls, bouncing, 2, 13
Baseball, 10
Batteries, 3, 4, 6
Bikes, 16–17
Bulldozers, 14

C
Cameras, 23
Cars, remote-control, 4
Climbing frames, 18
Computers, 8–9
Cranes, toy, 14

D
Dinghies, inflatable, 21, 30

E
Elastic materials, 5, 13, 31
Electrical circuits, 6, 30
Electricity, 4, 6, 7, 25, 30
Energy, 4, 5, 7, 11, 13, 30
Evaporation, 28, 31

F
Face paints, 28
Felt pens, 28
Film, camera, 23
Fluorescence, 23
Forces, 10, 11, 15, 21, 31
Friction, 10, 11, 16, 31
Frisbees, 20

G
Gear wheels, 16–17, 30
Glue, 29
Gravity, 12, 30

K
Kaleidoscopes, 22

L
LEGO, 14, 19
Levers, 15, 30
Light, 6, 22, 23, 30

M
Magnets, 6, 7, 31
Marbles, 12, 22
Meccano, 19
Model kits, 26
Modelling clay, 29
Motors, electric, 4, 7, 31
Music, 24, 25

P
Planes, model, 20
Pogo sticks, 5
Pulleys, 14, 30

R
Radio signals, 4, 24, 31
Recorders, 25
Reflection, 22, 30
Rollerblades, 11
Rudders, 21

S
See-saws, 15
Slides, 10
Sound, 24, 25, 31
Springs, 4, 5

T
Teddy bears, 26, 27
Tents, 18
Trains, electric, 7
Transparency, 22, 31

V
Virtual reality, 8

W
Walkie-talkies, 24
Wind-up toys, 4